YANNI ❧ ETHNICITY

"If our souls can come together in the music, they can come together anywhere–and so can we." —Yanni

"I'm inspired by anyone who has accomplished something that is extraordinary because it shows that anything is possible." —Yanni

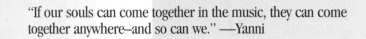

CONTENTS

ISBN 0-634-05704-9

HAL•LEONARD®
CORPORATION
7777 W. BLUEMOUND RD. P.O. BOX 13819 MILWAUKEE, WI 53213

www.yanni.com

Visit Hal Leonard Online at
www.halleonard.com

YANNI BIOGRAPHY

Yanni was born into a picturesque seaside village that no one ever gave thought to leaving and is now known in every corner of the globe. Yanni is, without a doubt, a musical phenomenon, one of those rare artists whose music defies borders and boundaries – whose music speaks to people of all races, all nations. And there is more than ample evidence to support such statements.

How many artists have become the favored composer of every Olympic broadcast for the past decade? Sold-out Radio City Music Hall for ten dates? Played in the shadow of the Taj Mahal, the Forbidden City and the Parthenon? Toured China and more than twenty other nations? Had a TV special seen in 65 countries by half a billion people, was one of the top fundraising artists of all time for PBS, and released what became the #2 best-selling live concert video? And, also mounted the #1-ranked concert tour for the first half of 1998.

Yanni is an artist that crosses all demographics in his appeal. Recently he returned to PBS with a new television special, Live At Royal Albert Hall, London, offering not only a spectacular concert appearance in this historic venue, but also the first glimpse into his family home in Greece and recording studio in Florida.

Virgin Records released Ethnicity in February, his 13th album and third on Virgin. Extending the "One World, One People" philosophy that has been the hallmark of his career, Ethnicity offers an upbeat collection of tracks that pulse with the rhythms and voices of cultures around the globe. Its instrumentation is equally diverse: from the aboriginal depth of the Australian didgeridoo to the haunting tone of the Armenian duduk – from the Celtic-flavored violin to the percussive plunk of the Indian tabla – the album brims with international flavor. The melodic sensibility of the album is unmistakably Yanni.

"Many of the world's cultures and musical genres are represented on this album. It has a lot of ethnic color – in other words, it has ethnicity," says Yanni. "Ethnicity has to do with race and culture, and – in the way I use it for this album – the color and beauty of a multicultural society. You can be proud of your heritage and still be part of a world community."

One element distinguishing Ethnicity from previous albums is the extensive use of human voices, not only solo arias and group chants, but also bona fide lyrics, a rare departure for the artist. "The Promise," for example, is an adaptation of an earlier composition, "Secret Vows," featuring lyrics from longtime friend Pamela McNeill and brilliantly sung by Alfreda Gerald, a member of Yanni's Tribute tour. The album's final track reflects his own cultural heritage with a traditional and very beautiful Greek island folk song, "Jivaeri."

After a five-year break from touring, Yanni began an ambitious 2003/04 world tour on March 1, at Mandalay Bay Resort in Las Vegas, featuring many of his new compositions and spotlighting the talents of solo virtuoso musicians the world over, along with his symphony orchestra. Miramax Books published Yanni's autobiography, Yanni In Words, a story that spans his fascinating and inspirational life from his childhood in Greece to his college years in Minnesota – to his success as an international superstar. The memoir, written in collaboration with David Rensin, also includes deeply personal details including his intense nine-year relationship with actress Linda Evans. It became a New York Times best-seller in its first week of release.

"I've been asked to write a book on many occasions but I was always focused first and foremost on my music and my career," said Yanni. "For the past few years I've had more of an opportunity to think deeply about life . . . I have tasted and felt so many things in my life and been welcomed all around the world. I have surpassed the wildest dreams I ever had as a child. I thought that now was the right time to talk about it. What better reason to write a book?"

Yanni has always charted a solitary and distinctive path. A champion swimmer and self-taught pianist with the gift of perfect pitch, he left the comforts of Kalamata, Greece, on the spectacular shores of the deep blue Mediterranean, and then began to fashion his own kind of American success story, later to become an international success story.

After graduating from the University of Minnesota with a B.A. in psychology, after trading the Grecian sunshine for frosty winters, he would seek a life in music, though he could not read a note and wrote wholly original works that, then and now, defy categorizing. From the beginning, he operated with a simple creed: a faith in hard work and keeping an open mind.

Yanni's first Grammy-nominated album was Dare To Dream (1992), which produced the vocal single "Aria," popularized by an award-winning British Airways commercial. His following album, In My Time, a gentler collection of piano-focused pieces, was also nominated for a Grammy Award and attained Platinum status.

In 1994 Yanni achieved a personal triumph when he returned to his Greek homeland and recorded an album at the 2,000-year-old Herod Atticus Theatre in Athens. The result, Yanni Live At The Acropolis, would be a sensation. It has almost continuously remained on the charts since its release, sold more than seven million copies worldwide, earned more than 35 platinum and gold albums, and has risen to become one of the best-selling music videos of all time.

How to follow the unprecedented success of Live At The Acropolis? By becoming the first major Western artist ever to perform at India's Taj Mahal and China's Forbidden City, resulting in the multi-platinum album Tribute. This is an artist who invested millions of dollars into the project before a single sound was recorded, whose organization mounted a near-biblical effort with the regional government of Uttar Pradesh to improve roads and build two bridges in order that the flood plains surrounding the Taj Mahal could be transformed for three historic concerts beneath one of the world's greatest wonders. While allowing India's citizens to see a musical performance in front of the country's signature structure, Tribute ultimately led to three million dollars in donations to a Taj preservation fund. The recording of Tribute proceeded to China, where Yanni staged a new historic feat at another of the world's great architectural achievements, the Forbidden City. Between India and China, Yanni played to a collective audience of 250 million people.

In 2000 Yanni released his first studio album in seven years, If I Could Tell You, an introspective and deeply personal project which came in the wake of a two-year sabbatical, a move to the east coast of the U.S., and other changes which refocused his life and life's work.

"Music," says Yanni, "is an incredibly direct language. It bypasses logic and speaks directly to your soul." It is this notion that inspired the boy who began his musical career by giving recitals before family members in a seaside village, and who has since been communicating on a global level that few of his peers can match.

RITES OF PASSAGE

Composed by YANNI

Moderately

FOR ALL SEASONS

Composed by YANNI

Very slowly, freely

Fast, steadily

To Coda ⊕

D.S. al Coda

CODA

Repeat ad lib. and Fade

Optional Ending

THE PROMISE

Composed by YANNI
Lyrics by PAMELA McNEILL

20

RAINMAKER

Composed by YANNI

Slowly, expressively

Moderately Fast, Steadily

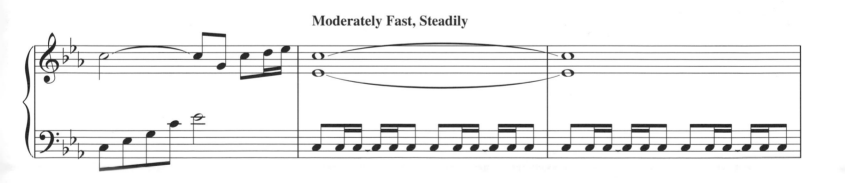

8vb

WRITTEN ON THE WIND

Composed by YANNI

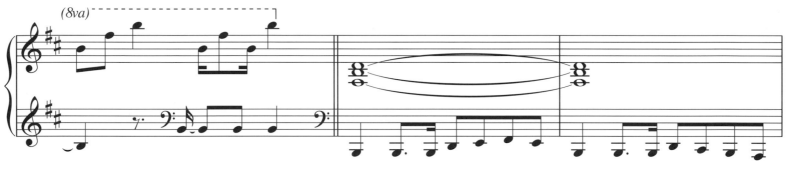

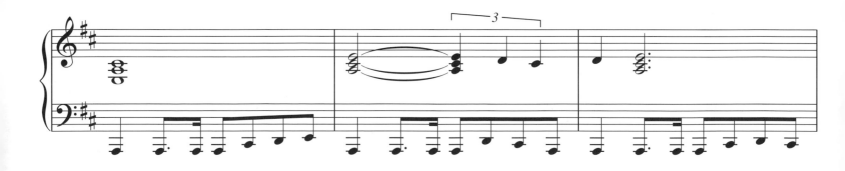

8va to end

Repeat and Fade

Optional Ending

PLAYING BY HEART

Composed by YANNI

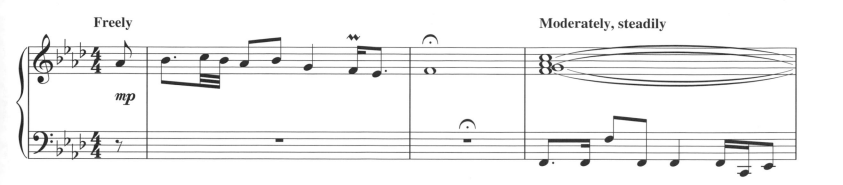

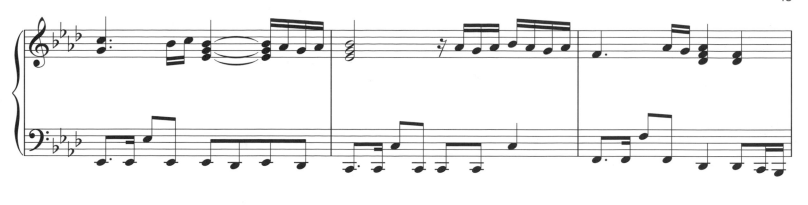

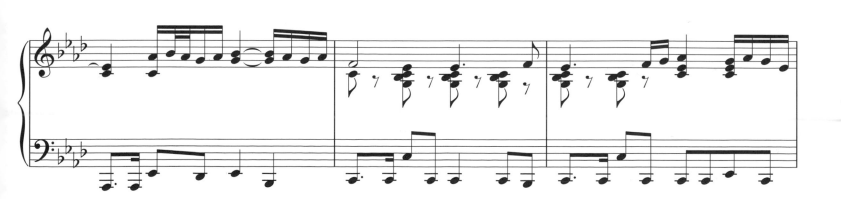

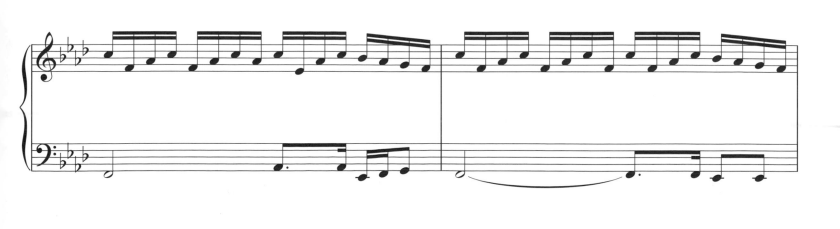

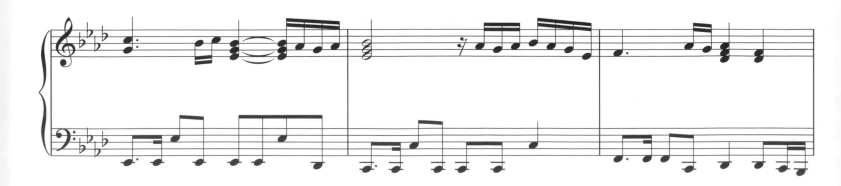

Repeat and Fade

Optional Ending

AT FIRST SIGHT

Composed by YANNI

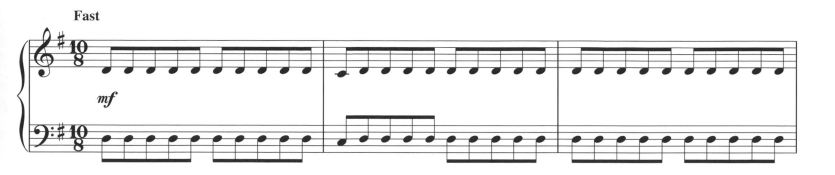

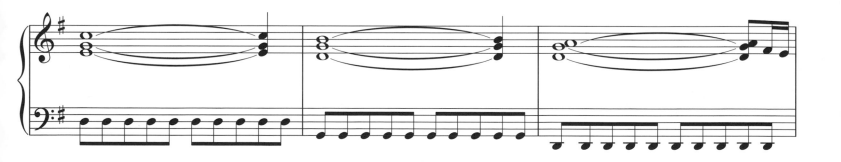

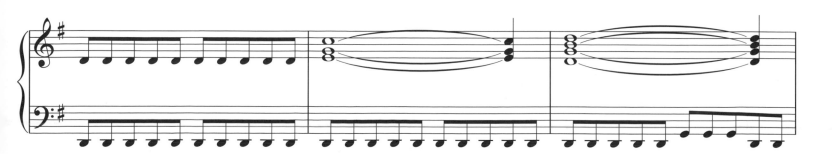

D.S. al Coda

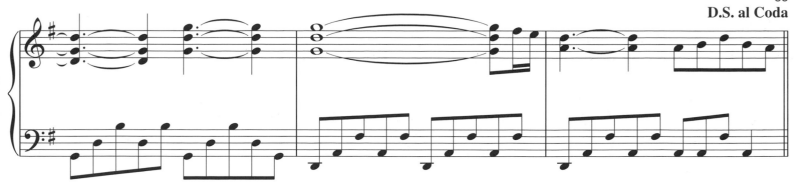

CODA

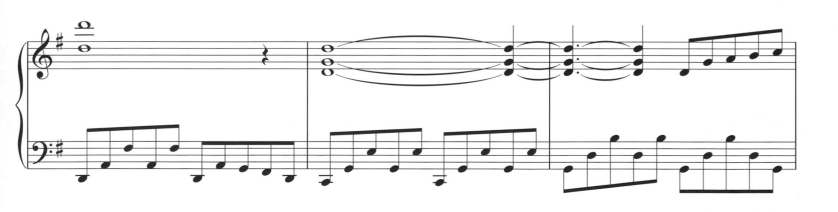

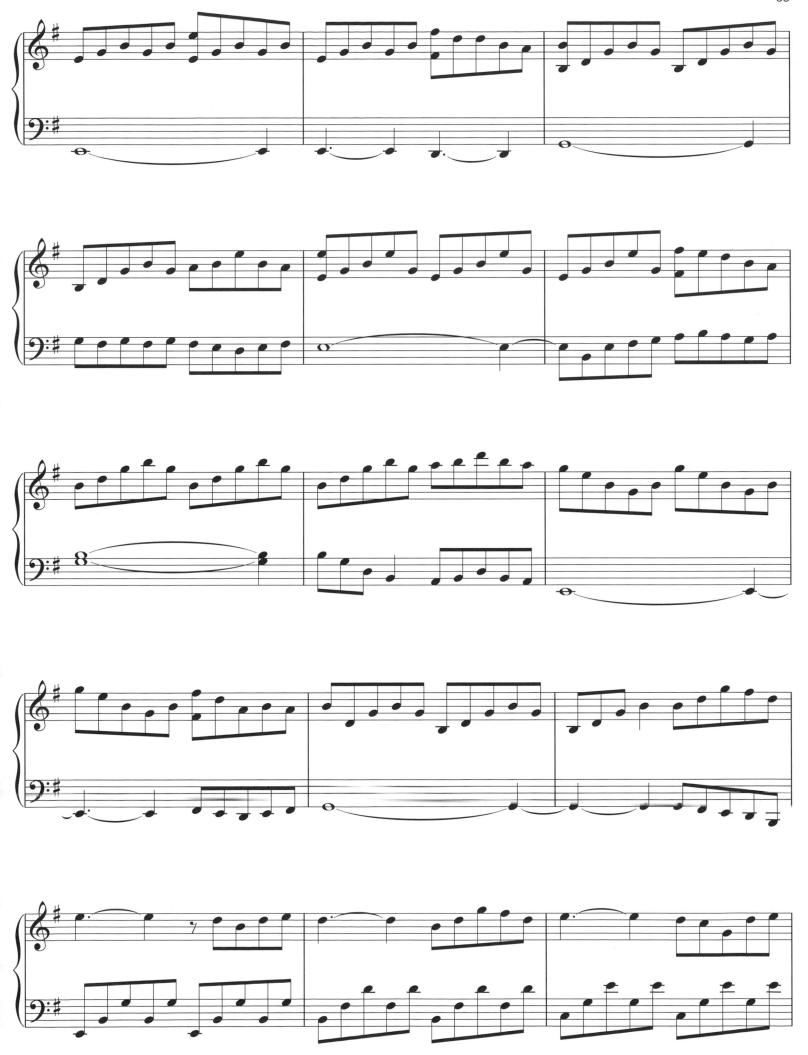

58

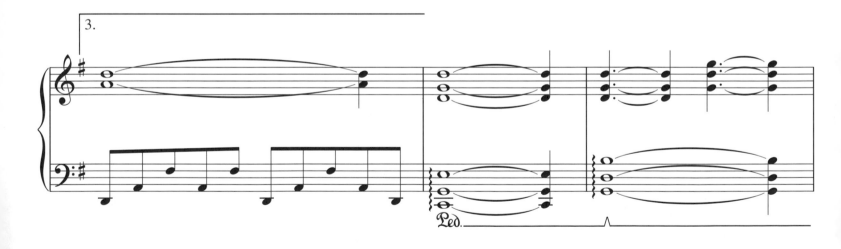

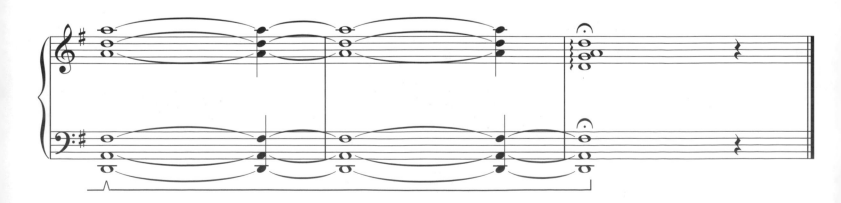

TRIBAL DREAM

Composed by YANNI

Repeat and Fade

Optional Ending

ALMOST A WHISPER

Composed by YANNI
Lyrics by PAMELA McNEILL

D   Bm   **D.S. al Coda**

To

CODA

A

in us. _____ The

F#m   Bm7

sound of hold - ing on,   al - most a whis -

F#m   D6

per. The sigh of bro - ken hearts, a qui - et

NEVER TOO LATE

Composed by YANNI

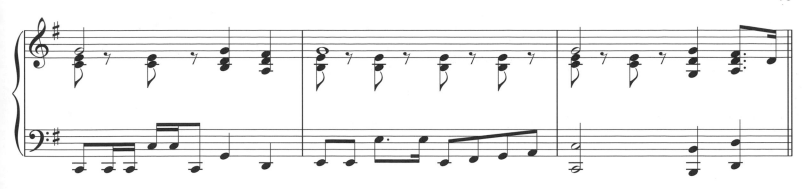

Repeat ad lib and Fade

Optional Ending

PLAY TIME

Composed by YANNI

Moderately Fast

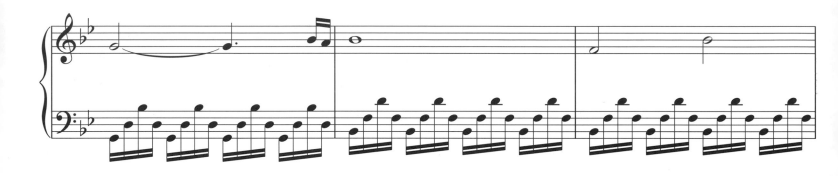

JIVAERI
(Jiva-eri)

Composed by YANNI

Slowly, expressively

Pedal ad lib throughout

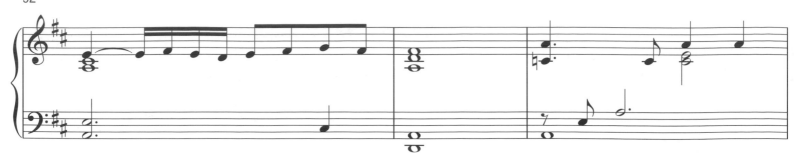

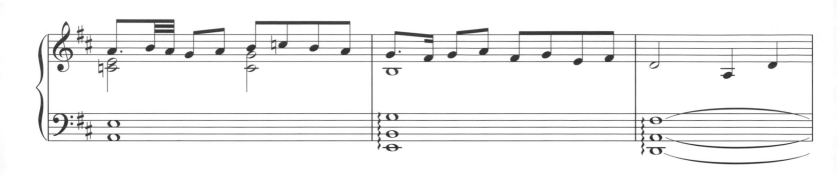

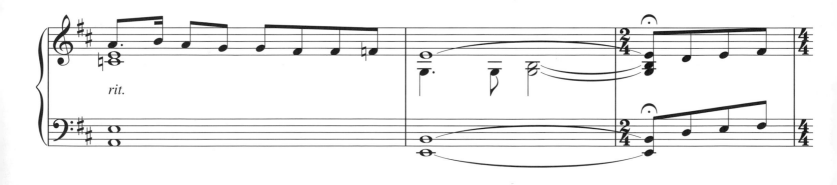

Steadily, slightly faster

To Coda ⊕